CALAFIORI

FOOTBALL AND LIFE

Inside the World of True Fans

By Pitt Anddy

INTRODUCTION

"Calafiori – Football And Life" invites you to explore the dynamic journey of Arsenal's promising left-back, Riccardo Calafiori. This meticulously researched and engaging book delves into the life and career of the Italian defender, tracing his impressive ascent from youth football in Rome to a key position at one of Europe's elite clubs.

Within the pages, readers will discover rare stories, significant encounters, and pivotal moments that have shaped Calafiori's professional and personal growth. The book recounts his early years in Italy and his seamless adaptation to the Premier League, emphasizing the attributes that have made him an integral part of Arsenal's squad.

"Calafiori – Football And Life" provides an intimate view of the player's life through thorough analysis, captivating visuals, and comprehensive interviews. Ideal for passionate fans and football enthusiasts alike, this book offers a detailed examination of one of Arsenal's emerging defenders.

Embark on a journey into Calafiori's approach to football, his tactical insights, and the dreams that inspire him to excel on the pitch. "Calafiori – Football And Life" celebrates his exciting career, highlighting the impact he is beginning to have at Arsenal and the broader football landscape.

TABLE OF CONTENTS

PERSONAL LIFE

⚽ Early Life: Riccardo Calafiori was born on 19 May 2002 in Rome, Italy. He grew up in a football-loving family which supported his early interest in the sport.

⚽ Family Support: Calafiori credits his family, particularly his parents, for their unwavering support throughout his career, driving him to training sessions and matches from a young age.

⚽ Football Idol: Growing up, Calafiori idolised Paolo Maldini. He admired Maldini's defensive skills and leadership, which inspired him to pursue a career as a defender.

⚽ Multilingual Abilities: Besides his native Italian, Calafiori is proficient in English, which has helped him adapt to playing in different countries and communicate with international teammates.

⚽ Passion for Music: Calafiori enjoys listening to a variety of music genres, with a particular fondness for Italian pop and classic rock. Music helps him relax before matches.

⚽ Video Game Enthusiast: In his free time, Calafiori enjoys

playing video games, particularly FIFA. He often competes with his friends and teammates, showcasing his competitive nature off the pitch.

⚽ Fashion Sense: Known for his stylish fashion sense, Calafiori enjoys experimenting with different outfits and often shares his fashion choices on social media.

⚽   Pet Lover: Calafiori has a pet dog named Luna, who is a frequent feature in his social media posts. He often shares pictures and videos of their time together.

⚽   Community Engagement: He is actively involved in community service, participating in charity events and youth football clinics in his hometown to give back to the community that supported him.

⚽ Favourite Cuisine: Calafiori loves Italian cuisine, particularly dishes like pasta and pizza. He often shares his culinary experiences on social media, showcasing his love for food.

⚽ Educational Background: Despite his football commitments, Calafiori prioritised his education, balancing schoolwork with his training and matches during his youth.

⚽ Overcoming Injuries: Calafiori has faced significant injury setbacks, including a serious knee ligament injury at 16. His resilience and determination to recover have been key aspects of his career.

⚽ Close Friendships: Calafiori maintains close friendships

with several of his childhood friends and former teammates. These relationships have provided him with a strong support network.

⚽   Travel Enthusiast: He enjoys travelling and exploring new places. His football career has allowed him to visit many countries, and he often shares his travel experiences with fans.

⚽   Role Model: Calafiori is seen as a role model by many young aspiring footballers. His journey from a youth academy to professional football inspires others to pursue their dreams.

⚽   Favourite Movies: He is a fan of Italian cinema and enjoys watching classic Italian films. His favourite movie is "La Vita è Bella" (Life is Beautiful).

⚽ 	Training Regime: Calafiori follows a strict training regime to maintain his physical condition. He often shares his workout routines on social media, inspiring fans to stay fit.

⚽ 	Social Media Presence: He is active on social media platforms like Instagram and Twitter, where he engages with fans, shares updates about his career, and promotes positive messages.

⚽ Hobbies: Apart from football, Calafiori enjoys reading and often shares book recommendations with his followers. His favourite genres include historical fiction and biographies.

⚽ Future Aspirations: Beyond football, Calafiori has expressed interest in pursuing ventures in sports

management and coaching.
He aims to leverage his
experience to contribute to
football in different capacities.

CLUB CAREER

⚽ Youth Development at Roma: Riccardo Calafiori joined the youth academy of AS Roma in 2010, where he developed his skills and grew into a promising young defender.

⚽ First Professional Contract: Calafiori signed his first professional contract with Roma on 16 June 2018, marking the beginning of his professional career.

⚽ Near Career-Ending Injury: On 2 October 2018, Calafiori suffered a severe knee injury that nearly ended his career. His determination and resilience saw him make a full recovery and return to the pitch.

⚽ Serie A Debut: He made his Serie A debut for Roma on 1 August 2020 in a 3-1 away win against Juventus. During the match, he won a penalty and scored a goal, though the latter was disallowed.

⚽ First Professional Goal: Calafiori scored his first professional goal for Roma on 3 December 2020 in a UEFA Europa League match against Young Boys, helping his team secure a 3-1 victory.

⚽ Loan to Genoa: In January 2022, Calafiori joined Genoa

on loan, where he made three appearances in Serie A, gaining valuable playing experience.

⚽ Move to Basel: On 30 August 2022, Calafiori transferred to Swiss club FC Basel on a permanent deal. He signed a three-year contract and became a key player for the team.

⚽ Debut for Basel: Calafiori made his Swiss Super League

debut for Basel on 9 October 2022 in a match against Lugano, which ended in a 1-0 defeat.

⚽ Return to Serie A with Bologna: On 31 August 2023, Calafiori returned to Serie A, signing with Bologna alongside his Basel teammate Dan Ndoye.

⚽ Switch to Centre-Back: Under Bologna's head coach Thiago Motta, Calafiori was transitioned from a left-back to a centre-back, where he excelled and emerged as one of the best players in the league.

⚽   First Serie A Goals: On 20 May 2024, Calafiori scored his first Serie A goals, netting a brace in a 3-3 draw against Juventus. His performance was a highlight of his season at Bologna.

⚽ Champions League Qualification: Calafiori played a crucial role in helping Bologna qualify for the UEFA Champions League for the first time since the 1964-65 season, ensuring a top-five finish in Serie A.

⚽ Transfer to Arsenal: On 29 July 2024, Calafiori joined Premier League club Arsenal on a long-term contract, marking a significant step in his career.

⚽ Youth International Success: Calafiori represented Italy at various youth levels, including U15, U16, U17, U19, and U21, showcasing his talent on the international stage.

⚽ UEFA Next Generation List: In 2019, Calafiori was included in The Guardian's Next Generation list, which highlighted the 60 best young talents in world football.

⚽ UEFA's 50 for the Future: In 2021, Calafiori was named one of UEFA's "50 for the Future," recognising him as one of the most promising young players in Europe.

⚽ Serie A Player of the Month: Calafiori was named Serie A Player of the Month for May 2024, reflecting his outstanding performances and contributions to Bologna's successful season.

⚽ First Team Experience at Roma: During his time at Roma, Calafiori made 10 appearances for the first team, gaining crucial experience in Serie A and European competitions.

⚽ Career Stats: As of May 2024, Calafiori has played a total of 69 club matches, scoring 2 goals and providing 10 assists, showcasing his contributions on both ends of the pitch.

⚽ Overcoming Adversity: Throughout his career, Calafiori has demonstrated remarkable resilience, overcoming serious injuries and proving his capabilities as a top-level defender in European football.

NATIONAL TEAM CAREER

⚽ Youth National Team Debut: Riccardo Calafiori made his debut for Italy's U15 national team in 2017, marking the beginning of his international career at a young age.

⚽ Progression Through Youth Ranks: Calafiori progressed through various youth levels, representing Italy at U16, U17, U18, U19, and U21 levels, showcasing his development and potential.

⚽ U17 European Championship: He was part of the Italy U17 squad that competed in the 2019 UEFA European Under-17 Championship, where Italy finished as runners-up.

⚽ Key Player in U17 World Cup: Calafiori played a crucial

role in Italy's U17 team during the 2019 FIFA U-17 World Cup, helping the team reach the quarter-finals.

⚽ U19 European Championship: He represented Italy in the 2021 UEFA European Under-19 Championship, gaining valuable experience in international competitions.

⚽ U21 National Team Debut: Calafiori made his debut for

Italy's U21 national team on 3 September 2021 in a friendly match against Slovenia.

⚽ Consistent Performer: Throughout his youth national team career, Calafiori has been known for his consistent performances, regularly contributing both defensively and offensively.

⚽ Versatile Defender: His ability to play as both a left-back and centre-back has provided tactical flexibility for Italy's youth teams, making him a valuable asset.

⚽ Leadership Qualities: Calafiori has often been entrusted with leadership roles within the youth teams, demonstrating his maturity and ability to guide his teammates.

⚽ First International Goal: He scored his first international goal for Italy's U21 team in a

European Championship qualifier against Luxembourg on 12 October 2021.

⚽ Tactical Adaptability: Calafiori's tactical intelligence and adaptability have allowed him to excel in various defensive setups, whether in a back four or as part of a three-man defence.

⚽ Mentorship: Despite his young age, Calafiori has taken on mentorship roles within the national team setup, helping younger players adapt to the demands of international football.

⚽   Physical Presence: His height and physical presence have been significant assets in international competitions, enabling him to win aerial duels and outmuscle opponents.

⚽   Technical Skills: Calafiori's technical skills, including his ability to deliver accurate crosses and play precise long balls, have been crucial for Italy's attacking transitions.

⚽   Resilience and Recovery: His resilience in overcoming injuries and returning to form has been inspirational for his teammates, showcasing his determination and work ethic.

⚽   U21 European Championship: Calafiori was

part of the Italy U21 squad for the 2023 UEFA European Under-21 Championship, further solidifying his status as a key player for the national team.

⚽ National Team Training Camps: He has regularly participated in training camps with the senior national team, gaining exposure to the highest level of international football.

⚽   High Work Rate: Calafiori's high work rate and relentless energy on the pitch have been vital in maintaining defensive solidity and supporting the team's overall performance.

⚽   Strong Communication Skills: His ability to communicate effectively with teammates and coaches has been an essential part of his role in the national team, ensuring proper coordination and organisation.

⚽ Future Aspirations: Calafiori aims to break into the senior Italy national team, with aspirations of representing his country in major tournaments such as the UEFA European Championship and the FIFA World Cup.

RECORDS AND PERSONAL ACHIEVEMENTS

⚽ Youngest Debutant in Europa League: Riccardo Calafiori made his UEFA Europa League debut for AS Roma at just 18 years old, showcasing his early promise and earning recognition as one of the youngest players to feature in the competition.

⚽   First Professional Goal: Calafiori scored his first professional goal for Roma in a Europa League match against Young Boys on 3 December 2020. This goal marked a significant milestone in his career, highlighting his offensive capabilities as a defender.

⚽   Overcoming Severe Injury: In 2018, Calafiori suffered a severe knee injury that almost ended his career. His remarkable recovery and return to professional football is a testament to his resilience and determination, earning him widespread admiration.

⚽   Part of Italy U17 European Championship Squad: Calafiori was a key player for the Italy U17 national team that finished as runners-up in the 2019 UEFA European Under-17 Championship, demonstrating his potential on the international stage.

⚽ Included in UEFA's 50 for the Future: In 2021, Calafiori was named one of UEFA's "50 for the Future," a list that recognises the most promising young talents in European football, underscoring his high potential.

⚽ Serie A Player of the Month: Calafiori was named

Serie A Player of the Month for May 2024, reflecting his outstanding performances for Bologna and his significant contributions to the team's success.

⚽ Golden Boy Nomination: His impressive performances earned him a nomination for the Golden Boy award, which is given to the best young player in Europe, highlighting his recognition among football's elite talents.

⚽   First Serie A Goals: On 20 May 2024, Calafiori scored his first Serie A goals, netting a brace in a 3-3 draw against Juventus. This performance was a highlight of his season and showcased his goal-scoring ability.

⚽   Transfer to Arsenal: On 29 July 2024, Calafiori joined Premier League club Arsenal on a long-term contract. This move to one of the biggest clubs in Europe marked a significant step in his career and reflected his growing reputation.

⚽ Key Role in Bologna's European Qualification: Calafiori played a crucial role in helping Bologna qualify for the UEFA Champions League for the first time since the 1964-65 season, ensuring a top-five finish in Serie A. His defensive solidity and contributions were vital to the team's historic achievement.

TECHNIQUE AND PLAYING STYLE

⚽ Versatile Defender: Riccardo Calafiori is known for his versatility in defence. He started his career as a left-back but has also excelled as a left-sided centre-back. This ability to play multiple defensive roles makes him a valuable asset for his teams.

⚽   Strong Defensive Skills: Calafiori's defensive skills are one of his key attributes. He is adept at making crucial tackles and interceptions, often disrupting the opposition's attacks and preventing goal-scoring opportunities.

⚽   Ball-Playing Ability: Calafiori is comfortable with the ball at his feet, showcasing excellent ball-playing ability. His passing range allows him to start attacks from the back, making him a crucial part of the team's build-up play.

⚽ Aerial Prowess: Standing at 1.87 metres (6 feet 2 inches), Calafiori is strong in the air. His height and timing make him effective in aerial duels, both defensively and offensively during set-pieces.

⚽ Physical Presence: Calafiori's physical presence is significant. His strength and athleticism enable him to outmuscle opponents, win physical battles, and maintain defensive solidity.

⚽ Aggressive Tackling: Known for his aggressive tackling, Calafiori does not shy away from challenges. His ability to win the ball cleanly and assertively adds a layer of security to his team's defence.

⚽ Tactical Intelligence: Calafiori possesses a high level of tactical intelligence. He reads the game well, anticipates the movements of opponents, and positions himself effectively to intercept passes and block shots.

⚽ Composure Under Pressure: Calafiori remains

composed under pressure, a crucial trait for a defender. His calmness allows him to make clear-headed decisions, maintain possession, and execute accurate passes even in high-pressure situations.

⚽   Crossing Ability: As a former left-back, Calafiori has developed an excellent crossing ability. His accurate and powerful crosses from the left flank create numerous goal-scoring opportunities for his teammates.

⚽   Leadership on the Pitch: Despite his young age, Calafiori has demonstrated leadership qualities. He often organises the defence, communicates effectively with his teammates, and leads by example on the pitch.

Printed in Great Britain
by Amazon

56234446R00031